Learning to Serve

Lord, make me an instrument of Thy peace;

where there is hatred, let me sow love;

where there is injury, pardon;

where there is doubt, faith;

where there is despair, hope;

where there is darkness, light;

and where there is sadness, joy.

O Divine Master,

grant that I may not so much seek to be consoled as to console;

to be understood, as to understand;

to be loved, as to love;

for it is in giving that we receive,

it is in pardoning that we are pardoned,

and it is in dying that we are born to Eternal Life.

Amen.

St Francis of Assisi

Contents

Introduction

This study guide is all about serving. It's not glamorous but it is fundamental to our faith. In fact, if I had to choose one aspect of Christian faith that was the most essential for us to pay attention to this would come second *[I'd put learning intimacy with our heavenly Father above it]*. I hope, that at the end of six weeks, those of you who use this guide will come away with a fresh sense of purpose in the lives that God has entrusted you with; an improved attitude to the tasks He calls you to; and a greater love for the people he gives you to serve.

There's a parable in Matthew's gospel *(ch. 25)* which is known as the parable of the talents. The master goes away and entrusts his servants with 5, 2 or 1 talents (a sizeable sum of money). On his return, those with 5 and 2 talents have doubled their money, while the one with 1 talent has buried it out of fear. While the one who buried the money has kept it safe, he hasn't done anything with it. The money is taken from him and he is thrown out of the master's estate. The two who double their investment are commended.

When the master commends the good servants he speaks to them like this:

> 'Well done, good and faithful servant! You have been faithful with a few things; I will put you in charge of many things. Come and share your master's happiness!' *Mt. 25:21*

I once heard Tony Campolo speaking about people he'd met in an old people's home. When looking back over their lives they all said they wish they had taken more risks. He enjoined us not to use 'take care' so readily as a parting greeting but 'take risks'. The problem with the bad servant in the story was that he was risk averse. I wonder whether many of us hold back from some new area of service to others because we're cautious. Caution doesn't lead to a good outcome in our story!

The adventure this course invites you to is one of risk. I once heard that faith was spelt R – I – S – K and there is some truth to that. The risk involved is in stepping out of our current comfort zones and venturing our all for the sake of the Kingdom of God and those who God calls us to. God is looking for those who will spend themselves on behalf of the world He calls us to. He calls us to go beyond just looking after ourselves first. God doesn't just want whatever we feel we have left after looking after our own needs – he wants the whole of us.

When Paul sends Epaphroditus back to the church in Philippi he commends him like this:

'Welcome him in the Lord with great joy, and honour men like him, because he almost died for the work of Christ.' *Phil. 2:29,30*

Epaphroditus gambled his life in a high-risk, high-return investment strategy for the 'work of Christ'. He, and others like him, will be welcomed into heaven with the words: *'Well done, good and faithful servant'*.

I hope that this course will allow you the chance to evaluate where you are in the business of spending your life for others. Perhaps there are some areas of service, whether at home, work or church where you can step out and say 'I don't know whether I can do this, but with God's help I'll give it a go.' I really believe that until we live a little beyond our natural inclinations and capacities, we'll never discover the power of God's grace to see us through.

There are several parables, like the parable of the talents, which describe our lives as a sacred trust. They ultimately belong to God, and he will want them returned and accounted for. For now, we are the stewards of all God has given us, and it is up to us to choose how to use them.

It really helps me to think like this – my life isn't my own, to squander as I wish, it belongs to God. One day I will give him an account of it. But for now, I have been given the awesome privilege of looking after it and making the most of it.

I hope that this course will help you reflect on how to make the most of whatever God has entrusted you with in this life. One day you'll need to explain it all to him. Will you work towards investing your life as best you can? If you will, you can be confident of the master's good report.

May God bless you richly,

Richard Morgan

How To Use This Guide

This guide is envisaged as a resource for those who are taking part in a group discussion about service each week, listening to teaching about service at the weekend services and setting aside some time for personal reading, prayer and reflection. Can I encourage you to commit to all three activities each week – each will reinforce the others. It will, however, also work as a stand-alone guide for personal study – and if the group you belong to is committed to some other topic for these weeks, please do use it for this.

So then, the components that you are invited to engage with are as follows:

Sermon Series

The studies in this book complement our six week weekend teaching series. You can listen online to sermons that accompany this series online at good-samaritan.org. The sermon dates are April 22nd, 2018 up until June 10th (May 20th and 27th are not in the series). We will do our best to get all the sermons online promptly after the Sundays (usually at some point on Monday) for anyone who wants to listen to sermons in the series that they have missed.

Comment

Each week in the guide begins with a comment from me, outlining our theme for the week. I hope these are helpful, but I don't mind one bit if you skip them all together. The purpose of any bible study guide is to draw our attention to the scriptures, not to provide us with a shortcut so that we don't bother paying attention to the texts themselves. Please regard the task as the careful (and prayerful) listening to the scriptures each week. The weekly comment is simply the equivalent of a cd's sleeve notes. It is not meant to replace or compete with the music itself and is entirely optional.

Personal Study

The personal study can be done before or after the group study. The question(s) and the space to scribble is to allow you to note what has come out of the scripture that you have read. Again, please use the space to write whatever notes and reflections are helpful. The job is not to answer the questions – it is to listen to what God is saying about your life through the scripture. If the questions help, very good. If not, just ignore them and write whatever is significant for you.

I think we can too easily rush reading the scripture and think about what it means or what we should do before we have really heard the passage. Can I suggest this as a method for reading:

- Take a few minutes in prayer just to bring the day to come before God – you'll be thinking about it anyway – so bring those thoughts to the Lord and seek his guidance and help.
- Then spend a minute or two in stillness. Be aware of the Holy Spirit's presence with you, and do no more than spend time in his company.
- Read the passage slowly.
- Then read it again – this time if it is teaching try and weigh each statement or sentence carefully, and reflect on it. If it is a story, then try and imagine the scene and the parts the various characters play in it.
- Then close your eyes. For teaching, allow yourself to chew over whatever has most struck you. For a story, re-run the story in your imagination. In both cases be attentive to whatever the Holy Spirits prompts in you as you digest the Word of God.
- Only now pay any attention to the question(s) in the guide. If they are helpful in clarifying and developing your thoughts then note your responses in the space given. If God has brought something entirely different to your attention then use the space to write that down instead.

Some of you are good at keeping diaries and journals. There will not be nearly enough space for you in this guide. Please write your copious thoughts somewhere else (in your journal?). Others will not be used to writing personal reflection at all. It is not obligatory. However, one or two bullet points will always be useful as an aide-memoire and to help clarify whatever it is that God is speaking to you through the passages.

Group Study

The group study passage should preferably be prepared in exactly the same way as the passages for personal study. You might want to leave a little space in the guide for reflections that strike you in the course of a discussion with others. Because we all approach texts differently, sometimes someone else will see something quite valuable to us that we would never have seen if only left to our own devices.

Your group study will be much more beneficial if you are all sharing your reflections about something you have prayed and thought about than if you are coming to the passage completely cold. Why not agree with one another that you will all 'do your homework'.

When you share with one another in the group, it is tempting to abstract the discussion from any actual consequences for my life, or any real incidences where I know I have fallen short. If we are able to always ask not just 'what does this mean?' but 'what does it mean for me?' and ground that in real stories of our lives, and real decisions that will shape our relationships going forward then we will have a much deeper fellowship and more profitable discussions.

To that end, I would encourage groups in the 'study' part of their evening to begin with a recap of last week's discussion and the opportunity to share what we did about it. In this way we hold each other accountable for our faith and life and can more effectively encourage one another.

Your discussions need not be very long, and I would hope that they would soon turn to prayer for one another that God may help you put into practice whatever you have learned.

Action

In James' letter, he says this:

> 'Do not merely listen to the word, and so deceive yourselves. Do what it says. Anyone who listens to the word but does not do what it says is like a man who looks at his face in the mirror and, after looking at himself, goes away and forgets what he looks like. But the man who looks intently into the perfect law that gives freedom, and continues to do this, not forgetting what he has heard, but doing it – he will be blessed in what he does.' *James 1:22-25*

Each week there is a space entitled 'Action'. It is for you to write down the things that you will **do**. They are, if you like, a space for a list of personal resolutions. Please fill them in at whatever point in the process of personal study, preparing for the group study or in the group discussions that they occur to you. Review them at the end of the week, and then perhaps also look back over previous weeks' 'action points'.

It is not intended that you share these action points with anyone, but you may well find that helpful. It may be that groups might like to break down into twos and threes for prayer, and that this would be an opportunity to share whatever 'action' decisions you have taken - so that you might pray for one another and then gently enquire on the subsequent week as to how things are going.

Prayer

There is a prayer at the end of each week's study. Sometimes in the course of a study like this one I like to prayer a prayer like this each day at the end of a quiet time. I read the text quickly, then think of how it might apply to me as a real cry of my heart to the Lord, and then I pray through the text of the prayer allowing it to be the occasion of bringing my relationships and resolutions to God in prayer. By using the same text each day, I allow a pattern of prayer to form within me, and find that prayer strengthened as the week goes through.

Week One

It's not all me, me, me

Our course begins with the extraordinary truth that if we want to find our lives we need to lose them. What is Jesus on about?

All of us long to live meaningful and purposeful lives. We want to live lives of significance. Jesus expresses something of that longing in the human heart when he says 'I have come that they might have life, and have it to the full'. I wonder whether we feel that we have lives that are being lived 'to the full'? What would that look like?

As soon as we ask ourselves about our own lives we start navel gazing. What would make me happier? What would make me more useful? What would make me feel I'd fulfilled my potential? It's all about me, me, me.

I have a lot of sympathy for the 'me' question – many of the 'me' questions we will ask are quite genuine and maybe even altruistic. The problem is, that once the focus is all about me, we can quickly find ourselves horribly at odds with God's thinking about a situation. Think of Peter's reaction when Jesus first foretold the crucifixion: 'Never, Lord... this shall never happen to you'.

Jesus' answer is very radical. He says, if we want to discover that full life, we need to start by giving up on the 'me, me, me'. The beginning of the journey is to deny ourselves and follow him. Those who will lose their lives 'for him' will find them.

It's a big deal for us to move the focus from ourselves to Jesus.

The challenge of this week is to ask ourselves whether we believe Jesus. Will giving up our ego, our desires, our wants really take us to the place of blessing, fulfilment and happiness. It's counter-intuitive. If we're going to trust him, then the next think is to begin to align our thinking with this key Kingdom value. What does it mean to stop thinking 'me' and start seeing everything through the lens of letting go of self, and following Jesus?

Personal Study 1

John 10:1-18

Are you are living the 'full' life that Jesus meant for you? What would an abundant life look like?

How do you recognise the shepherd's voice day by day?

Jesus says that the good shepherd 'lays down his life for the sheep'. Do you think that God calls you to 'lay down your life' too? If so, are there any particular things that he is calling you to at the moment?

Personal Study 2

Matthew 19:16-30

The Rich Young Man of the story was very serious about living a good life. Why was that not enough?

If you're brave enough, ask Jesus the question 'If I want to be perfect what should I do?' What is the answer?

Peter is very honest in asking whether his 'self denial' policy really has a payoff. Try being that honest with God too. What do you expect God to give you in return for following him? Do those expectations need re-shaping?

Group Study

Matthew 16:21-28

What are my ambitions in life?

Are they my ambitions for me, or are they Jesus' ambitions for me?

What stops me from being selfless?

If I'm to follow Jesus, I need to hear his voice. How do I?

Action

Write down any of the things that need to change in your life and what you are going to do about them:

Prayer

Thanks be to thee, my Lord Jesus Christ,
For all the benefits thou hast won for me,
For all the pains and insults thou hast borne for me.
O most merciful Redeemer, Friend and Brother,
May I know thee more clearly,
Love thee more dearly,
And follow thee more nearly,
Day by day.

Richard of Chichester

Week Two

Greatness is found through Service

The most extraordinary funeral I ever took was of a hospital cleaner in Bath. She lived in a very ordinary house, and had a very ordinary job. There would have been nothing on her CV to mark her out as any different from any other hospital cleaner.

Her family's attitude to the funeral was that if it was good enough for the Queen of England it would be good enough for their mother. They hired a horse drawn hearse which was brought from the East End of London to Bath (I don't even want to think about what that cost) and walked behind it for the mile or so from their house to the church. The horses were huge and black with plumes on their heads which raised their stature further; the hearse was ornate, yet dignified. The Queen of England would have been proud.

It took more than quarter of an hour to get the standing room only crowd into the church. I had never seen so many people in the church building. She had not even died especially young – she was in her 60s – young enough to draw a decent group of friends and family but nothing to explain the scale of the crowd that had come to pay their respects.

The secret was unveiled in the tribute given by one of the family. He said that he had had difficulty contacted people about the funeral because of this lady's address book. It wasn't organised by surname, nor even by first name. Family members would be under 'O' – for 'our Anne, our Peter' etc… Roger would be under 'S' for 'Sarah's Roger' and so on. He described the book as a book of relationships.

People had mattered to this hospital cleaner from Bath. She knew them, loved them and cared for them.

Her life was not significant because of her qualifications, but out of the quality of her relationships.

Jesus says that the secret to this kind of greatness is learning to serve others.

Personal Study 1

1 Timothy 6:17-19

Where does your 'status' come from. What things (money, things you are proud of) give you a sense of security?

Where should I put my trust? Are there particular things that I need to learn to trust God for?

Our wealth should come in 'good deeds'; we should be generous and willing to share. That's how we take hold of the 'life that is truly life'. What are the good deeds and generosity that God is challenging you about today?

Personal Study 2

1 John 3:16-20

What is the example of Jesus that we are to follow? Who is it that God is calling you to lay your life down for *(why not write their names down)*?

Does your love for other people ever stop with 'words and tongue'? Is there someone today you need to love in 'action and truth'? What do you need to do?

How are our actions connected to our relationship with God and the effectiveness of our prayers?

Group Study

Mark 10:35-45

What do we want God to do for us?

James and John were in for a different future than the one they might have imagined. The cup and baptism that Jesus has in mind refer to his death, not glory. When has God taken us places that we did not think we wanted to go?

How would people in the world in general measure greatness?

How does Jesus measure greatness? What is the challenge for us?

Action

Write down any of the things that need to change in your life and what you are
going to do about them:

Prayer

O my God, teach me to be generous:
To serve you as you deserve;
To give and not to count the cost;
To fight and not to heed the wounds:
To labour and not to seek to rest;
To give of myself and not to ask for reward,
except the reward of knowing that I am doing your will.

Ignatius of Loyola

Week Three

Doing what need doing

An attitude of service means being prepared to get stuck in doing whatever needs doing. While there may be some ways in which we serve other people that require qualifications or gifting *(I don't want my heart operation carried out by a surgeon with a great attitude but no skills)* most of the ways in which we can serve others are basic and mundane. More than that, serving someone in a basic way with the right attitude *(gladly, expecting nothing in return)* communicates and gives much more than just the act itself. Think about when you have received great 'service' at a restaurant – didn't it make the whole meal more relaxed and the experience more enjoyable?

In the famous passage at the end of Acts 2, it says that the believers *'gave to anyone as he had need'*. In fact the business of providing for people's needs had become so time consuming that by Acts chapter 6 the Twelve realise that they cannot organise it and appoint seven men 'full of the Spirit and wisdom' to take over this essential role. We can tell the importance given to this role, because the seven are all named and when they are chosen, the apostles commission them with prayer and the laying on of hands.

We may not be called to be the administrators of a major food distribution program like those seven were. We can have the same attitude of service, though. 'Full of the Holy Spirit and wisdom', we too will be equipped to see others as Jesus sees them, and to reach out to them in acts of loving service.

Community members coming to the end of their time at Lee Abbey would share their experience of community at their last community meeting - and people would respond. It was a positive time, and the person leaving was encouraged – 'we loved your humour / your friendship / your great cooking' etc... Just sometimes, though, people would say 'having you around was like having Jesus with us'. It never referred to great preaching, miraculous signs or amazing prophetic gifts. It always spoke of character. The people who were not full of themselves; who looked out for other people. The people whose lives were full of small, mostly unnoticed and undistinguished, acts of service. Those who quietly got on with doing what needed doing.

Personal Study 1

Romans 12: 9-18

Note some of the things that all Christians are called to in this passage:

How can you 'honour others above yourself'?

'Do not be proud, but be willing to associate with people of low position. Do not be conceited.' Are there some tasks *(or people)* which we feel are 'beneath us'. What might they be?

Personal Study 2

James 2:14-26

Am I ever tempted to think of faith as something interior, and separate from the way that I live?

'Faith without actions is dead'. If you were on trial for being a Christian what evidence would there be to convict you?

What practical needs do other people have that God is calling you to meet?

Group Study

John 13:1-17

Why does Simon Peter not want Jesus to wash his feet?

What menial tasks do you regularly avoid?

Imagine Jesus washing your feet? How do you feel?

'you should also wash one another's feet' – what can I do to fulfil that instruction?

Action

Write down any of the things that need to change in your life and what you are going to do about them:

Prayer

I am no longer my own, but thine.
Put me to what thou wilt, rank me with whom thou wilt.
Put me to doing, put me to suffering.
Let me be employed by thee or laid aside for thee,
exalted for thee or brought low for thee.
Let me be full, let me be empty.
Let me have all things, let me have nothing.
I freely and heartily yield all things to thy pleasure and disposal.

From John Wesley's Covenant Prayer

Week Four

My gifts are for other people

We need a fundamental attitude of being willing to serve others. That need we share with all other Christians. However, as well as sharing a common calling, God has also made each of us unique. Each of us has a set of characteristics and abilities which make us who we are. In the parable at the beginning of this booklet one servant is given one talent – another five. We are not accountable to God for whether we are super-talented, or rather less talented. We're accountable for what we do with what we've been given.

As well as having a set of gifts and abilities that we got at birth, God is also able to give us gifts above and beyond these. Paul encourages us to 'eagerly desire spiritual gifts' *(especially the gift of prophecy)*. We need to pray for ourselves and for one another that God would increasingly release these spiritual gifts to us – and we need to seek them.

We don't seek to develop any gifts (natural or spiritual) for their own sake. Tempting as it is to want a whole raft of spiritual gifts just to convey to us a sense of God's presence and blessing that's not what they're for. Paul is clear when he teaches us that God gives us gifts 'for the common good' *(1 Cor 12:7)*. The purpose of the gifts that God gives us is to build up and serve one another. We're not called by God as individuals but as part of a body. As part of that body we need to remember that 'each member belongs to all the others' *(Rom 12:5)*.

It's important for us to recognise the gifts that God has given us, and to get on with using them for the sake of others.

Personal Study 1

Romans 12:1-8

What are the fundamental attitudes described in the first two verses which underpin the description of different gifts in the section which follows.

Who do I belong to according to this passage? How do I express that?

Do you recognise any of the gifts in this list? What gifts has God given you?

Personal Study 2

1 Corinthians 12:1-31

Who arranged the parts of the body? What part has God given you in the Body of Christ?

What are the responsibilities of each part of the body to the others? What does that mean for me?

Has God given you any of the gifts in this list in Corinthians? What are the gifts that you 'eagerly desire'?

Group Study

1 Peter 4:7-11

What are the instructions that are given to all the people that Peter writes to? How will they help us in our common life?

What gifts have we been given?

Whose strength should we serve in? How do we do that?

Are there practical steps we need to take to become more faithful in 'administering the grace that God has given us'?

Action

Write down any of the things that need to change in your life and what you are going to do about them:

Prayer

Dear Jesus, help me to spread Thy fragrance everywhere I go.
Flood my soul with Thy spirit and love.
Penetrate and possess my being so utterly that all my life may only be a radiance of Thine.
Shine through me and be so in me that every soul I come in contact with may feel Thy presence in my soul.
Let them look up and see no longer me but only Jesus.
Stay with me and then I shall begin to shine as you shine, so to shine as to be a light to others.

Daily Prayer of Mother Teresa

Week Five

Others First, Me Second

In the garden of Gesthsemane, the night before the crucifixion, Jesus prays an extraordinary prayer: 'not my will, but yours be done'. In contrast to the many prayers we pray asking God for what we want *(i.e. – 'my will please be done')* Jesus' prayer is a cry for his Father's purpose to be worked out in his life. He understood that his life was for the sake of others.

When he speaks to his disciples on the way to that garden he teaches them like this:

> 'My command is this: Love each other as I have loved you. Greater love has no one than this, that he lay down his life for his friends'
> *John 15:13,14*

The example of Jesus in the garden is not just for him – it's a pattern for us to follow. It works itself out in our lives exactly at the point when we begin to prefer God's will to our own. And by choosing to put God's will first, we inevitably find that those he calls us to take precedence over our own agendas and ambitions.

It's when we're prepared to live with this radical re-orientation of our priorities that we find ourselves in the place of God's purposes for our lives, and so also in the place where we discover that he is able to work in us and through us.

While it may sound trite, the Sunday school acronym that Nicky Gumbel quotes in 'Life Worth Living' has a truth to it:

J – Jesus first
O – Others second
Y – Yourself last

Our challenge this week is to look to commit the whole of ourselves to serving God's purposes, not our own. As we do that, we need to trust him to provide for us and strengthen us. Only once we start to live beyond ourselves will we really discover the truth of what Paul wrote when he said '[Jesus] was crucified in weakness, yet he lives by God's power. Likewise, we are weak in him, yet by God's power we will live with him to serve you' *(1 Cor 13:4)*.

Personal Study 1

Mark 12:28-34

Why is the command to love God first, and the one to love our neighbour second?

How do I develop and strengthen the love I have for God?

What does it mean for me to 'love my neighbour as myself'?

Personal Study 2

Galatians 5:7-10

What things am I doing which are 'sowing to please the sinful nature'? What I am doing to 'sow to please the Spirit'?

When do you 'weary in doing good'.

Who should we 'do good to'? Who are those people in your life?

Group Study

Philippians 2:1-11

What motivates us to serve others?

What things are we tempted to do out of 'selfish ambition or conceit'?

What does it mean to 'consider others better than yourself'?

As we read this description of the attitude that Jesus had, what is the personal challenge to you?

Action

Write down any of the things that need to change in your life and what you are going to do about them:

Prayer

Stir our hearts on fire with love to thee, O Christ our God,
that in its flame we may love thee with all our heart,
with all our mind, with all our soul and with all our strength,
and our neighbours as ourselves,
so that keeping thy commandments,
we may glorify thee, the giver of all good gifts.

Eastern Orthodox Kontakion

Week Six

How to keep going

One of the problems people face with a life lived for other people is how to keep going. Sometimes people commit to great service of other people for a season only to find themselves emotionally drained or burned out.

Living to the full – emotionally, physically and spiritually is draining. That's why Elijah found himself on Mount Horeb. He'd had enough. That's why God needed to take him to one side and speak to him.

We can only effectively serve other people out of the love and strength that God pours into us. It's why we need to put our relationship with God first, before even our love of our neighbour.

If we try and serve out of a sense of duty or obligation we become resentful and tired very quickly. Part of not living in a self-centred fashion will be learning not to regard ourselves as so important that people can't do without us. We need to learn to serve from a place of freedom – serving people out of love, not because we need to be needed.

Even when we live out of a place of closeness to God, we get tired and in need of refreshment. When we serve out of love, not out of guilt we will be able to step aside at the right time from the busyness we are engaged with to rest and spiritually re-fuel.

I love the response that Mother Teresa gave when she was asked when she was called to serve to poor. She said that she had never been called to serve the poor. She'd been called to follow Jesus and he'd led her to the poor. If we can get that priority right in our lives, then we will find ourselves always serving from a place where we are strengthen and renewed by him.

The promise Isaiah gives is for each of us:

> 'Even youths grow tired and weary, and young men stumble and fall; but those who hope in the Lord will renew their strength. They will soar on wings like eagles; they will run and not grow weary, they will walk and not be faint.' *Isaiah 40:30,31*

Personal Study 1

Luke 10:38-42

What is the one thing needed?

When are you tempted to put the busyness of what needs doing before your relationship with Jesus?

Are there any things that I need to put into place in my life to get it back in balance?

Personal Study 2

Mark 1:29-39

What is the pattern of activity and spiritual retreat that Jesus demonstrates here?

How does spending time in prayer shape what Jesus does next?

How do you build in time for retreat and prayer into your life? Do you need to re-assess this?

Group Study

1 Kings 19

When have you felt like Elijah when he says 'I've had enough Lord'?

In those times, how has God renewed you?

When has God most powerfully spoken to you?

What do we learn about keeping going in serving from this passage?

Action

Write down any of the things that need to change in your life and what you are going to do about them:

Prayer

Lord Jesus draw me close to you.
Fill me with your Holy Spirit this day.
Pour your love into my heart,
and let it flow out into the world you call me to.
Keep me from relying only on myself,
But help me to trust you.
Where I am empty, fill me.
Where I am weak, strengthen me,
Where I am broken, heal me.

Notes for Group Leaders

Each of you will structure a whole evening for your groups. There will be testimony, worship and praise. You will have time for ministering to one another with the laying on of hands and time for intercession. There will be space to catch up on previous weeks and to encourage one another in your faith. There will be room for refreshments and general chat. To allow all these essential things to take their proper place, I would encourage you to be reasonably crisp with the 'study' or 'Word' part of your session.

I have found it helpful to bookend this kind of study with an icebreaker at the beginning and pray in 3s or 4s at the end. The icebreaker is as much to introduce the theme as to break any ice. It's been helpful in groups I have taken, though, to get people to think through what an issue really means to them in some way or other so that when they open their Bibles they are connecting what they read with real life, and not with just talk. Prayer in very small groups (even pairs?) allows people to pray very specifically, and also allows a bit of scope for some checking up on 'progress so far'.

In the discussion using this booklet, please don't feel obliged to cover all four questions of an evening. It may well be that it is enough for each group member to share something from their preparation that has especially challenged them. For some groups a particular theme might emerge – go with the flow.

Here are some 'icebreaker' suggestions for each week:

Week One (It's all about me, me, me!)

Ask people to think about who the most self-centred person they have ever come across is. They will need to share quite quickly if you are to go round the whole group. It would be enough for just a few people to contribute.

Week Two – Greatness is found through Service

What is your best experience of service in a restaurant? What was it that made it special?

Week Three – Doing what need doing

What is your least favourite domestic chore? What do you hate about it?

Week Four – My gifts are for other people

Ask the group when people first really experienced the Holy Spirit.

Week Five – Others First, Me Second

What is the most selfish thing that you have ever done?

Week Six – How to keep going

Where's your favourite place to go to spend time with Jesus?

Made in the USA
Columbia, SC
03 April 2018